PORTFOLIO 9

METROPOLITAN SEMINARS IN ART

Portfolio 9 · *Techniques*

by John Canaday

ART EDITOR AND CRITIC
THE NEW YORK TIMES

THE METROPOLITAN MUSEUM OF ART

TECHNIQUES
Tempera and Oil

THIS PORTFOLIO is concerned with the painter as a trained workman, a view that is not very popular today in certain art circles. The layman retains a nostalgic idea of the artist as an individual trained to a high degree of skill in a specialized job. But he receives very little sympathy from the modernist, who is more likely to think of an artist as an individual with a gift of expression so important and so urgent that it must be released at any cost; certainly, the modernist would say, at the cost of skills that take time to learn and may dwarf or stifle his unique gift in the learning. The gift of expression, we deduce, is more vulnerable to dwarfing and stifling today than in previous centuries, for the old masters were able to maintain it in healthy condition during rigorous apprenticeships lasting a period of years.

The old masters were trained to the standards of their craft. When they had mastered the craft, they put it at the service of their patrons' requirements without feeling any loss of creative integrity. But the modern painter has been put in the opposite position—he paints for himself and then offers his work for sale. By comparison with the old masters he is a fabricator of spectacular novelties who seeks to impose his personality upon the susceptible in the hope that they will buy.

The tendency to be downright suspicious of any contemporary painting executed with concession to traditional craftsmanship is based upon the erroneous assumption that the demands of craftsmanship are antipathetic to expressive individuality. Now, if it were necessary to choose between pure craftsmanship without expression and pure expression without craftsmanship, no question would be involved. The function of painting is expression. But it should not be necessary to make this choice. In the great painting of the past it is not even possible, because expression and craftsmanship are so fused that they cannot be divorced from one another.

The attitude of suspicion toward technical proficiency germinated about a hundred years ago under legitimate circumstances. In the middle of the nineteenth century the painters of the then all-powerful French Academy attached exaggerated importance to technical facility. It was possible for a painter who was clever with his brush (and shrewd or fortunate in his connections) to dominate the official Salons with the most trite and obvious interpretations of trite and obvious subjects. It was a rosy era for the established hack. The Salon juries were the arbiters of taste, and the buying public was delighted to receive unimpeachable confirmation that the pictures that appealed to them in such familiar terms were the great works of their time. The layman has seldom been party to so happy a coincidence in such matters.

An example of academic Salon painting at its slickest was included in our first portfolio when Pierre Cot's *The Storm* (Plate 11) was compared to its disadvantage with a modern

5

painting by Oskar Kokoschka, *The Tempest* (Plate 12). There cannot be much question about which of these is the more important expressive work, and Kokoschka's painting also happens to be technically sound.

Revolt against the Academy was inevitable in a country where aesthetic sensibility is indestructible. It came from the first radically "modern" artists, the impressionists, who are now the most familiar and best-loved painters in this hemisphere. The impressionists were skillful technicians, but they were not conventional. Their freedom and originality appalled the Academy and reduced to confusion a public indignant at having the rug pulled out from under them. The impressionists carried the day, however, and their success has stimulated further departures by succeeding generations until the violation of convention has become for second-rate painters an end in itself.

Craftsmanship as Expression

The purpose of our preamble is to introduce a contention heretical in terms of contemporary art criticism; to wit, that the craft of painting may be not only a means to expression, as anyone would admit, and not only an integral part of expression, as we said a few paragraphs ago, but may even constitute in itself a major form of expression. To illustrate, we have reproduced the *Madonna and Child* (Plate 97) by Tommaso da Modena, painted in the fourteenth century. This little picture is the left half of a diptych whose two parts are hinged to close together face to face like the pages of a book. It is a kind of portable shrine painted, no doubt, so that some wealthy and devout person might carry with him on his travels an image of the Madonna and of his patron saint, Jerome (*Figure 1*).

In neither of these figures—and certainly not in that of the Child, which is only a pretty manikin—has Tommaso exercised any particular originality, force, or emotional depth of conception. These are honest, respectably executed figures invested with whatever qualities are appropriate to the Madonna and Saint Jerome, but they appeal more by ready-made associations than by any special interpretation given by the artist. The Madonna bends over the Child in an attitude that is adequately tender but entirely in the formula of countless other figures of the Madonna painted by Tommaso's contemporaries. The Child is thoroughly disappointing if we try to find anything inherently more profound than a doll-like prettiness. The little spindles of bright-colored thread are an engaging detail and an attractive bit of ornamental pattern (*Figure 2*). Saint Jerome's lion, squeezed into a corner like an afterthought, resembles a tabby cat more than the king of beasts.

And yet the picture is intensely expressive. It glitters with gold and precious pigments applied with an exquisite elaboration that becomes devotionally expressive in itself. It is as much a jewel as a painting; the craft of the jeweler, in fact, overlaps the craft of the painter in such a work. The background is a film of pure gold applied in thin sheets and highly burnished, so that in its original condition the picture appeared to be painted on a solid panel of that rich metal. This background is elaborately and delicately tooled with a marginal pattern made up of a multitude of small indentations that catch the light (*Figure 3*). This enrichment is repeated in the halos. Around the Madonna's halo the aureole flames gently where the surface of the gold has been indented in a series of radiating lines. The Madonna's gown is a sumptuous brocade of yellow paint and gold metal. The entire gown was first painted and modeled in yellow; then the pigment was scratched away in a pattern, revealing the pure gold of the panel. This gold pattern, in turn, was tooled with minute indentations that not only increase its richness but, being as delicate as threads, give the gold a brocadelike texture and differentiate it from the flat gold of the background. Otherwise it might appear that the background was show-

Figure 1

ing through holes cut in a pasteboard figure. Over his thigh and along his back the Child's robe has been treated with a variation of the same technique. First the whole robe was painted blue, then modeled with tiny scratches that once again reveal the gold background in strokes like those of a pen or fine-tipped brush, so that the robe takes form and turns golden simultaneously.

As the picture is examined in detail it becomes apparent that it is shot through with gold in hundreds of tiny details. Gold is conspicuous along the ornamental borders of the Madonna's robe, but it also sparkles less obviously in the band of mosaic behind her. It appears in such small details as the stripes on the cushion upon which she is seated and even on the heads of the tassels. A gold filament runs through her veil, and there is an almost microscopic highlight of gold on the bobbin of white thread. All this rich detail is more than ornamental. It becomes devotional in character. In its psychological effect it is remindful of shrines covered with offerings of jewels, flowers, and trinkets from grateful worshipers.

The Craft of Egg Tempera Painting

Tommaso da Modena's *Madonna and Child and Saint Jerome* is an unusually pure example of painting in the egg tempera technique, which was in general use well into the fifteenth century when it began to merge with the new developments in oil technique. The methods of the old masters were not static; there was a process of growth in which each generation of painters added new devices or capitalized on new pigments and binders to extend the means of expression. The history of painting is a double history in which new techniques parallel the expression of new philosophical concepts. In this portfolio we will follow the development of painting techniques over several centuries with the two ideas in mind: explain-

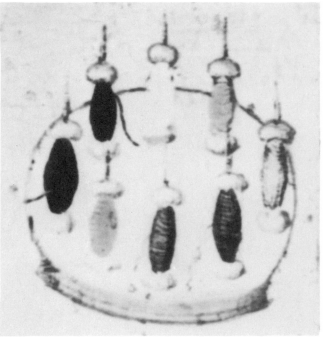

Figure 2

ing enough of the artist's way of working to enable the reader to understand how the pictures were painted and showing how these techniques were linked with the expression of the ideas of the time.

This approach was suggested in the preceding portfolio when we said that the breadth, amplitude, and nobility of fresco demanded

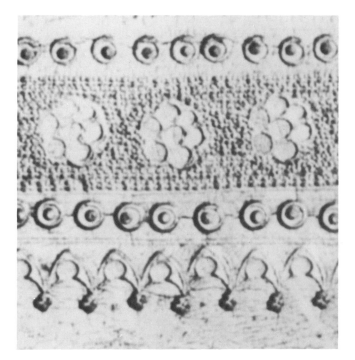

Figure 3

8

corresponding qualities in the painter. Fresco is so direct and vigorous by its very nature that it dictates ample, forthright forms that have a way of turning hollow and ponderous if they

produce a painting of expressive significance. In executing the *Madonna and Child* Tommaso did little more than follow conventional patterns for his figures and use to maximum

Figure 4

are not in the service of a philosophical ideal large enough to merit their use.

By contrast we have just seen in an egg tempera painting a technique so precise, so delicate, so absolutely controlled in minutiae that it may become an end in itself and still

advantage the kind of small, ornamental details that in fresco are impossible, pointless, or inappropriate. Fresco is merciless in its revelation of any shortcomings of a painter. Tempera is demanding in another way. It requires of the artist extreme precision, control, and patience. It is slow. It does not allow for suggestion; the area of a large painting must be covered as meticulously as that of a small one. But it rewards the artist with a tolerance for statements of secondary importance. Some of the greatest pictures in the world, the great pictures of the early Renaissance, were painted in pure egg tempera, but this is also, of all the periods of painting, the one in which minor masters appear to best advantage. Even the painter who did not have a great deal to say was likely to say his little bit with order and clarity. Even the painter with nothing at all to say, if he managed to become a painter at all, was able to turn out pictures that offer at least the satisfaction inherent in a well-made object.

To appreciate egg tempera painting as a technique we must abandon the picture of an artist standing before his easel at work on a canvas, improvising to a certain extent as he paints, covering large areas rapidly with a stout brush, manipulating pigment as he pleases, smoothing it, blending it with other colors, applying it thickly or thinly as seems best. We must visualize instead a painter at a workbench applying color in small, thin strokes that dry immediately. And he is at work not on a canvas but on a panel whose preparation in itself has involved a degree of craftsmanship. When he was an apprentice the artist helped prepare panels in the master's studio. As he proceeded in his training he was allowed to work on more and more important stages of the many through which an egg tempera painting progresses on its way to completion. As he grew more proficient he was allowed to paint some of the preliminary passages or even to execute some of the minor figures in the master's commissions. He would eventually paint entire pictures under the master's instruction, and by these degrees he would attain recognized status as a full-fledged painter in his own right, ready to set up his own studio and train other apprentices in the technique.

Preparing the Panel

Several stages of the production of a large egg tempera panel are revealed in the *Madonna Enthroned between Saints Peter and Leonard* (Plate 98), executed about the third quarter of the thirteenth century by a painter of the Florentine school. It is a highly stylized work of the same general period and character as the painted cross (Plate 35, Portfolio 3) on which we commented in connection with expressionism. The comments made there apply to this painting also, as far as its expressive character is concerned. The Madonna is enthroned between Saint Leonard (left) and Saint Peter, with six scenes from the latter's life introduced along the sides. But our concern here is the unusual nature of this panel as an examination piece in the craft of egg tempera painting from the very beginning, the preparation of the wooden panel, to its completion. The original panel is exposed in the lower part of the picture, whereas in other areas the painting is in nearly perfect condition. Between these two stages all the intermediate ones are seen.

When it came into the possession of the museum where it is now exhibited, the panel had experienced the normal history of very old pictures that have suffered from alternating periods of neglect and attention. Parts of it had disappeared and been restored with varying degrees of skill. Other parts had been damaged and repainted. Modern laboratory methods, including X-ray and chemical analysis, can determine with a good degree of certainty the difference in age between the original painting and restored portions of such a panel. (On the surface, they may appear to be indistinguishable if the restorations have been good ones.) In this case, the technicians removed, fragment by fragment, every bit of matter thought to have been added to the original work. Film by film, the layers of varnish and dirt were removed until all that remained of the original surface was exposed.

Normally the next step would have been an

Figure 5

11

accurate rebuilding of the missing portions and a scholarly and technically accurate restoration of the surface, a process that in the right hands can virtually re-create the original. In this case, however, the panel has been left at the intermediate stage as a study piece.

The accompanying detail shows in actual size the area below the hem of Saint Leonard's gown (*Figure 4*). The shred of linen visible on the right is a bit of the piece that originally covered the entire panel, not only to strengthen it but also to serve as a base for a layer of gesso, upon which the actual painting is done. Gesso is an extremely fine-textured, brilliant white substance, like plaster but bound together by glue instead of the lime that limits the fresco palette. Gesso cannot be substituted for plaster in fresco painting for several reasons: it is not easy to prepare in large quantities, it dries too fast for true fresco technique, and it lacks the lime binder. An entire wall could be gessoed, but quite aside from time and expense it would not be practical. The virtue of gesso as a painting surface is that it allows the painter a wonderfully smooth, brilliant panel upon which he can do work of great delicacy intended for the kind of close-range examination not ordinarily given to large surfaces of wall decoration.

Gesso is applied to the panel in several layers that are allowed to dry between applications. It is brushed on like paint while it is in a warm, fluid condition. (Since one of the ingredients is gelatine, it hardens upon cooling.) When a thickness of an eighth of an inch or so has been built up, the gesso is allowed to harden thoroughly and is then sanded. The resultant surface is comparable to the smoothest eggshell and is a joy to paint on. It accepts paint readily but has just enough tooth to act as a slight brake that helps the painter control his brush.

The Craft of Gilding

If, like the examples we have just seen, the tempera painting is to include passages of gold,

the gilding must precede any painting. In the passages where gold is to be applied the gesso is lightly covered with gilder's clay, which serves as an adhesive for the gold leaf and, more importantly, as a base for the necessary burnishing. Gilder's clay is brick red in color—handsome in itself. Applied like thin paint and built up in several filmy layers, it is allowed to dry, is burnished to a smooth gloss, and then dampened a bit. Then it is ready to receive the gold.

Gold leaf is the pure metal beaten into uniform tissue-thin leaves that, touched with the finger, disintegrate into fine powder. But a skillful gilder, using a wide, flat, brushlike instrument called a gilder's tip, can pick up sheets as large as three inches square. The gold leaf is attracted to the hairs of the gilder's tip, but is more strongly attracted to the dampened surface of the red clay when brought close to it. If the craftsman is skillful or lucky, the leaf goes on in one piece; more often, cracks or holes appear in it, one reason why several applications are necessary to get a solid coverage. Each layer is burnished with a smoothly polished agate tool before the next is applied.

As, with time, the layer of gold evanesces slightly, the reddish tint of the gilder's clay shows through. It is particularly apparent in the area around the aureole of the Madonna in the painting by Tommaso da Modena. Fortunately the rich color of the clay is compatible with gold, and these reddish areas, showing through the surface of virtually all gilded panels as old as the ones we have seen, have a handsomeness of their own.

With the leaf laid on and burnished to satisfactory richness the panel is ready for whatever tooling it is to receive in halos, borders, or other areas. An examination of the border of the panel of Tommaso's *Madonna and Child* shows that the pattern is made up by the recombination of a few elements. The punching is done with small tools, frequently carved from bone, a few inches long

Figure 6

and comparable in other dimensions to knitting needles. One end has a pattern; it is rested on the surface of the gilded gesso, and the other end is given a firm tap. Inexpertly delivered, this blow may chip the gesso, a disaster. Our detail shows that, at most, half a dozen simple shapes have been combined to create a variety of patterns. Identifiable are a hollow circle, repeated seven times to make the center and the six petals of the flowerlike figure running along the central band, a half-circle and two arcs that are combined to make the lacy border along the inner edge, a simple blunt punch producing a miniature crater, and perhaps one or two others. The tooling can, of course, be done after the painting is completed, but it is ordinarily done first because less is lost if the panel cracks.

Except for occasional minor details egg tempera paintings are never improvised on the panels. Before the panel is touched by paint a drawing at full scale is completed. The preliminary drawing, called a cartoon, is finished in all its outlines and modeled in its more important areas. To transfer the outlines to the panel the usual practice is to scratch them lightly into the gesso surface. These scratched outlines can be seen here and there in a great many paintings if you search for them in a favorable light, even though they have become partially obscured by layers of paint.

Modeling in Tempera

Once the outlines are scratched in, it is at last time to apply color. Egg tempera paint is composed of approximately equal parts of powdered pigment, yolk of egg, and water. When used in the correct amount egg is a perfect binder. If there is too little of it, however, the pigment will powder off when it dries. If there is too much, the paint is gummy and hard to work with and has an unpleasant sticky-looking gloss when dry. An experienced painter can tell when the mixture is right by stirring it with his brush. The paint is mixed in

Figure 7

very small quantities—thimblefuls or, at most, spoonfuls at a time, since not much is required to cover a surface, and it tends to thicken and dry in the dish.

Using very small, pointed brushes the artist applies the paint stroke by stroke, not in washes or in broad areas. It dries instantly, at least as far as workability is concerned. The only way to apply a solid area of color is stroke by stroke until hundreds of crisscrossings produce a uniform flatness.

In our Tommaso da Modena the robe of the Madonna has not been modeled, a curious circumstance in a picture so wonderfully complete in all other passages, but a convenient omission for our purposes here. The scratched-in guide lines that were to have served Tommaso in modeling the robe in tones lighter and darker than the local color can be seen in our reproduction.

Modeling, like flat color, must be built up little stroke by little stroke until the form emerges. But difficulties increase at this point. Whereas the solid tone can be built up by crisscrossing lines in any direction, the modeling must "follow the form." Dürer's famous drawing *Hands of an Apostle* (*Figure 5*) explains this phrase. The hands are modeled entirely in line, without any recourse to flowing, blending, or smudging in the light and dark areas. The lines describe the complicated form of the hands by appearing, as it were, to

14

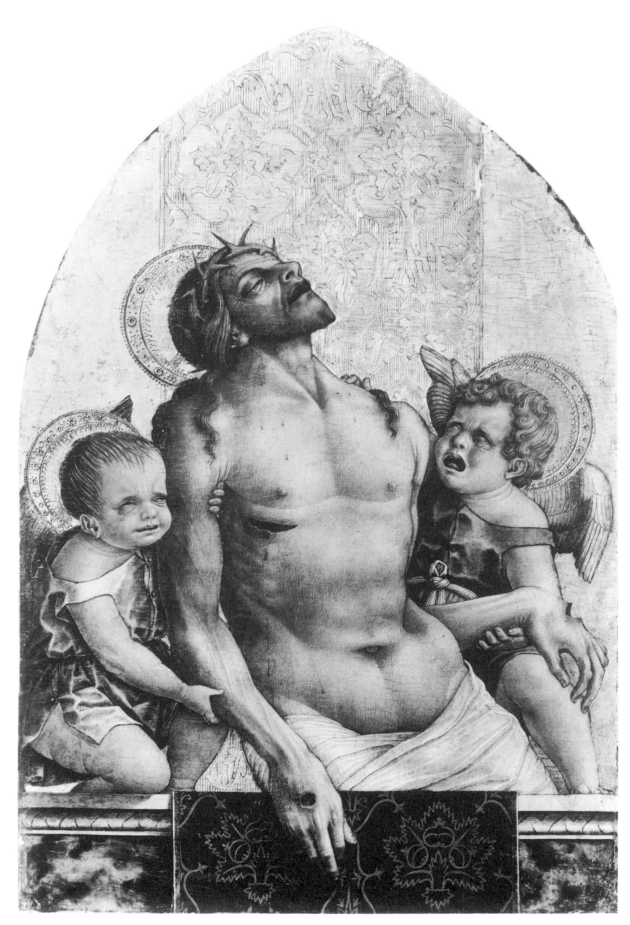

Figure 8

15

lie upon the part of the form they describe. The result is a double definition: once in terms of light and shade, as the eye sees form and as the camera records it, and once in terms that could be called diagrammatic. It is a powerful way of describing form, but a technically demanding one. A misplaced line would be immediately disfiguring, looking like a piece of wire or string projecting from the form instead of a descriptive line following it.

A painter may "follow the form" by cross-hatching as Dürer does or by using lines in only one direction, as Ghirlandaio does in the head of a little boy (Plate 99), which is reproduced at exact size from the double portrait *Francesco Sassetti and His Son Teodoro* (*Figure 6*). The modeling is rather shallow; the forms are treated more like a low sculptural relief in color than like three-dimensional forms existing in full depth surrounded by air. The red cap especially is very lightly modeled, and the delightful design of curling hair is conceived as much as a linear pattern as a three-dimensional form, so that it falls somewhere between the two. In addition to modeling the forms in only one direction, Ghirlandaio has reduced them to their simplest bases, in contrast to the method Dürer used in his drawing of the hands, in which he sought out intricacies and revealed them in multiple description by modeling in two or more line systems crossing one another on the same surface.

The greenish cast so frequent in flesh passages painted in tempera is the original base color showing through the superimposed modeling. The tempera formula for painting flesh areas is an exception to the rule that the entire part is first covered with a base tone of the object's local color. Tempera flesh tints modeled over a pink or cream base tone appear chalky and lifeless. Inasmuch as the dominant color in flesh tones is red, its complementary, green, is used as the base tone because it has a maximum vibration in opposition to red. In this way the flesh takes on greater liveliness from the minute variations of greenish base

tint that show through. The green tone was frequently left showing fairly obviously along the "shadow edge" where the light tones merge with darker ones, but seldom to the extent to which we so often see it now. Over the centuries the top film of paint tends to evanesce or grow more transparent. Virtually every tempera painting has been varnished, which also increases transparency. In addition, any cleaning that is carried a microscopic fraction of an inch too far further reveals the green base, so that in many tempera paintings the flesh areas have taken on an unhealthy pallor. The green is strong in the face of the Madonna in the Tommaso da Modena, in spite of the bright pink with which her cheeks are spotted. It can also be seen in Sassetta's *Saint Anthony Tempted by the Devil* (Plate 78, Portfolio 7), which is a beautifully executed little tempera painting in all its passages.

Ghirlandaio was a deft craftsman, and in *Francesco Sassetti and His Son Teodoro* he is painting at the top of his customary precise, almost mechanical performance. But as he is a rather literal-minded painter, our pleasure in this double portrait is visual more than anything else. With the usual allowance for associative factors having to do with the affection between father and son, the picture is essentially a handsome decoration in which the likenesses of two individuals figure.

Technique and Expression

The expressive force of Mantegna's *Adoration of the Shepherds* (*Figure 7*; in color, Plate 82, Portfolio 7), of which we reproduce a detail at full size (Plate 100), utilizes the strengths peculiar to the egg tempera technique with a vigor only hinted at in the preceding paintings.

Andrea Mantegna was one of the most vehement artists in the history of painting. Like all great creators he combines within his individual and perfectly unified conception a host of elements we would otherwise think of as contradictory or incompatible because they

16

are not fused similarly in the work of other men. He is a painter of the most intensely minute detail, yet no detail exists for itself alone. These details are as ornamental in their design as the best work in any decorative craft, yet their ornamental character never exceeds their expressive purpose. Mantegna represents scenes of brutality and anguish in acutely tangible forms cease to be fragments of the real world and become, instead, the integrated parts of a visionary one. His synthesis becomes magical through the very force of the exaggerated actuality of its component parts.

The Adoration of the Shepherds takes place in a world of stony ledges where feathery

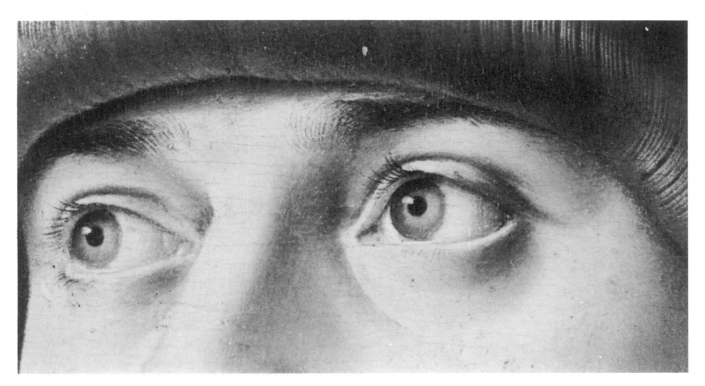

Figure 9

forms as hard as agate and as merciless as a knife, yet so impeccably finished that their violence is balanced by elegance. The forms he paints suggest sculpture in polished stones of fantastic color, so much so that it is usual to compare his work to carving and to remember that he filled his studio with Roman fragments; yet one no sooner recognizes this sculptural quality than the same forms that suggest it reassert themselves as superlative painting in terms of color and linear contours. Detail by detail Mantegna is an unyielding realist, whether he is representing a fold of cloth, a portion of the body, the growth of a leaf from its stem or a branch from the trunk of a tree, or a sprinkling of pebbles on the rocky ground. Yet in juxtaposition Mantegna's clouds float behind blasted trees. Gigantic rock forms slash into the sky. In the foreground the shepherds approach the miraculous Child where he lies in the folds of the Madonna's robe, which is spread around her on a ledge like an altar or a stage. Its harsh sides suggest a cliff, just as the rounded form stretching from it in the immediate foreground could be a mountain. One of the shepherds is represented as a reverent oaf. His companion, coarse and brutalized, seeks to comprehend what he half senses. But behind these half-animals in their ornamental rags a ruined tree sends delicate new branches into the air, and around the Madonna and Child hover cherubim painted in crimson and gold. The final effect of the picture is one of absolute motionlessness; even the air seems distilled of all movement. Every object, every twig or leaf and every fold of cloth is transfixed within the miracle.

In progressing from Tommaso da Modena's *Madonna and Child* to Mantegna's *Adoration of the Shepherds* we have run a gamut from a beautifully tooled little picture where craftsmanship carries the burden of expression to a masterpiece where expression is a matter of highly individualized conception, and the fusion between masterly conception and masterly craftsmanship is complete. We can take it for granted that Mantegna would have been a great painter in any technique. It stands to reason that if he had painted a hundred years later, or if he painted today, the almost compulsive force of his art would have found expression in different terms. But he happened to paint when tempera was the most highly developed technique, and he adapted it to the expression of his spirit in such a way that it is difficult to imagine him painting otherwise. The essence of his hard-bitten art is the invention and detailed description of expressive forms, which, in a general way, is true of all painters. In the case of Mantegna, however, it has specific application. When we examine the full-size detail of Saint Joseph sleeping, we feel first of all the impact of its expressive power; secondarily, we may become fascinated by its technique; we never see the painting as technique only. The technique is so unrelentingly directed toward expression in *The Adoration of the Shepherds* that to study it as technique is still to be affected by its expressive statement.

"Subtlety" may seem a curious word to use in connection with Mantegna when we have insisted on his intensity, but the word's appropriateness becomes apparent if we compare his art with that of a near contemporary, Carlo Crivelli. His *Pietà* (*Figure 8*), of which we reproduce a detail in color at a fraction over actual size (Plate 101), is a typical performance by Crivelli. He exaggerated the device of modeling in line within decisive con-

tours to the point of eccentric stylization and forced emotional expression to the point of affected hysteria. This sounds like a harsh description, but it is not intended to deny Crivelli's distinction. He is a superb craftsman and a painter of arresting pictures, but there is no point in pretending that in comparison with Mantegna he is anything more than a performer who has perfected a brilliant act. Mantegna is frequently violent, never blatant; always intense, never high-strung. Crivelli's shortcoming lies in his exaggeration of qualities we have described as virtues in Mantegna. His appeal must be to those who are willing to accept stylized hysteria for its own sake or to students who can find him interesting not so much for what he says as the way he says it. He is a good example of the kind of painter who takes on interest as part of a tradition, whereas he might have had none as an isolated phenomenon. He is included here as a kind of postscript to our consideration of tempera painting.

In the capacity of a postscript he is an important artist. In the relationship between technique and expression the arts of Tommaso da Modena and Crivelli demonstrate an ultimate contrast: the first paints with an innocent, unanalyzed conviction that craftsmanship itself endows a work with expression, the second on the sophisticated principle that technique can replace true expressive forms and create emotion where there is none.

Tempera and Texture

The artists we have seen so far in this portfolio have been working under the discipline of a technique that makes no concession in certain quarters in which the painter could otherwise extend his range of expression. Textures, for instance, are impossible to represent in tempera except within a narrow range. The way a robe falls, in delicate folds or in large ample ones, may indicate that it is supposed to be of a light material like thin silk or a heavy one

Figure 10

like thick wool, but there is no completely satisfactory way in tempera to simulate the difference between the sheen of silk and the nappy look of wool. While tempera is wonderfully suitable for the description of form it is not suitable for reproducing the quality of light as it is caught in different ways by different surfaces. Flesh passages painted in tempera, no matter how skillfully done, never take on the quality of flesh, but remain some harder, sharper substance tinted approximately the color of flesh. Fur (difficult to represent in any technique) is impossible in tempera. Individual hairs may be picked out neatly but the soft mass cannot be represented in a technique where the choice is between crisp line or mushy compromise. For instance, a bit of fur is introduced on the collar of the saint in Tommaso's *Madonna and Child and Saint Jerome*, but nobody is likely to grant the artist credit for anything more than a laudatory try at achieving the impossible.

Tempera is an art of clearly defined edges; objects cannot fade into shadow nor loom up from it. It is most effective in the upper color range. Dark colors tend to grow heavy and turgid. Tempera is also essentially an art of small scale. The huge altarpieces painted in it may seem to refute this statement, but a large tempera painting is simply an accumulation of close-range material assembled upon a large surface, a large amount of close-range painting. Dash, sweep, and free movement over large areas intended to make their effect from a distance are foreign to its nature. And the paint is a uniform film over the surface of the gesso; it cannot be piled up dramatically here, nor thinned out suggestively there. This is largely because tempera's medium is a "lean" one. A "fat" medium dries more slowly and allows the painter to brush in one area, pull another into it while it is still wet, blur an edge if he wishes, and to model by blending one tone with another instead of making the transition in a multitude of graduated tones. A fat medium can be piled thick or scrubbed thin, and it can run the entire range from black to white without loss of brilliance.

Oil Painting

The standard fat medium is oil. Oil as a binder for pigment was known long before it was much used by artists. The rarity of fine oils

Figure 11

20

might have had something to do with it. Still, rare and valuable pigments were in use. It may be that oil was not a popular medium because its degree of viscosity was not easy to control in mixtures of sufficient purity to assure its stability. Whatever the reason, oil as an adjunct to leaner techniques began to appear hesitantly and then flowered suddenly in the art of the Van Eycks, who capitalized to the full on its brilliance, its variety and range of color, and its smooth gradations from tone to tone. In our first portfolio we saw one of Jan van Eyck's great achievements, the double portrait of Giovanni Arnolfini and his wife (Plate 10, Portfolio 1). The gentle spread of light that unifies this composition could not have been much more than approximated in egg tempera technique.

From North European workshops knowledge of the new technique spread to Italy, where the Venetians took it up with particular enthusiasm. Bellini's *Portrait of a Young Man* (Plate 102), a painting from the transitional period when the range and brilliance of oil was grafted to the precise definition of tempera, should be placed next to the portrait of young Teodoro Sassetti for comparison. Both reproductions are the exact size of the originals.

Bellini's surface is still extremely smooth, and his drawing is sharply defined. He has not realized oil's potential for suggestion, as later painters will. But the advantages he has already gained are immediately apparent. The head with its cap of hair (still as formalized as in tempera) exists in three dimensions in vivid light, modeled in full range from brilliant highlights to dark shadows; by comparison, Teodoro's profile is a silhouette. The difference in the modeling around the eyes is particularly striking (*Figure 9*). In the Bellini the eyeball has a luster and transparency accounted for, again, by the artist's freedom to run the range of color from black to white and to capture the object's texture by imitating the kind of shadow edge and the value relationships of colors in close approximation to the way they actually appear in nature.

Although we do not know with any certainty the details of the technique, early oils like this one were apparently executed in glazes of pigmented oil over an underpainting in a leaner technique, tempera or perhaps a tempera-oil emulsion. This underpainting defined the forms in considerable detail, then brilliant, transparent oil glazes were used to "dye" them to the desired color. Obviously, there was a great deal of manipulation of the oil films, but their brilliance and variety is accounted for by the fact that they could be used essentially as dyes over an established form, if we want to define the fundamental principle involved.

Oil, Light, and Textures

The way was now open for the painter to see and paint in terms of light reflected upon the surface of forms instead of in terms of form alone. The climax of the concept of a painting as a textural symphony was reached two centuries later in the art of Vermeer, whose *Artist in His Studio* we saw in Plate 37, Portfolio 4. But in a detail of three figures (Plate 103) from Simon Marmion's *Crucifixion* (*Figure 10*), painted in 1470, we have an early example in which the painter attempts what amounts to a textural catalogue, with considerable success.

The three figures represent the three continents then known to Europeans, Europe, Asia, and Africa. The figures are pure fantasy, since the painter could have no clear archaeological references for the armor of a Roman soldier, the trappings of an Eastern chieftain, or the even more mysterious costume of an African warrior. The Roman is an exercise in the rendering of metallic lusters, including chain mail. But the East was associated with the idea of luxurious stuffs and Africa with that of the irrationally exotic, so the painter has invented for his Asian a costume of fur, brocade, silk, suede, gold, and gems, and for his African a costume of bizarre design full of

21

slicings, tuftings, and curious folds. For the Asian figure three furry textures are simulated —the long, silky, springy fur of the hat brim, the short-haired white fur of the collar and the hem of his jacket, and the very soft, loose texture of the warrior's own hair and beard. The purple velvet cloth of his jacket is contrasted with the shinier crimson velvet of his brocaded blouse, with harder-surfaced metallic threads setting off both these silky textures. No real gold is used in this painting; its color and texture are simulated in paint. Suede boots, a stiff leather scabbard, a brooch of pearls serving as a clasp at the side of the jacket, a belt studded with polished metal, and the ornamented handle of the sword, and a curious little tuft of folded linen complete the design, this last the end of his turban, projecting from the over-cap of fur and heavier cloth. The African's costume is made of lighter material, again accented by the glint of metal and jewels at the collar and in the ear, climaxing in a conical headdress of a texture fantastic enough to suggest that, all other textural possibilities being exhausted, the painter invented a new one. All these textures are played against the large contrast of hard rocks and the soft growth that partially covers them.

Oil Techniques
in the Renaissance

Both the Bellini and the Marmion retain the smooth surface of pure tempera, and like tempera they are painted on gessoed panels. Oil painting as most people think of it, a freer application of paint with visible brush strokes and a generally more eventful surface of varying thickness, developed gradually from this early hybrid. In Venice, particularly, the taste for luxuries on the grand scale was sympathetic to a more effulgent style of painting than the small-scale, tightly controlled renderings we have been seeing. In the next century the development came to a climax.

Titian's *Venus and Adonis* (*Figure 11*) is conceived to appeal first of all in sensuous terms. It relays the very feel of flesh, hair, silken gauze, jewels, foliage, and swirling, balmy air. By comparison Marmion's textures are an abstract exercise. *Venus and Adonis* is a large picture—it takes a large area to accommodate so opulent a conception so opulently painted— hence considerable reduction must be accepted in our detail (Plate 104) to include a variety of the textures and their play against one another. But even so, it should be apparent that now the texture of the paint itself is involved in simulating the textures of the various materials. Titian's paint is luscious in itself. Its texture is part of the picture's expressiveness just as form and color are.

In spite of its contrast to earlier paintings, the technique of *Venus and Adonis* is still based on underpainting that defines essential forms and on overpainting in glazes that tint and develop them. The underpainting is now done on canvas of a natural brownish color. The shadow areas are defined in darker golden browns painted thinly with fluid pigment; the lights, in a heavy white paint that may be piled up to considerable thickness. When the underpainting was dry the overpainting was built up on it in a series of colors and tones that might be produced not by a glaze of one color alone but by a whole series of glazes applied one on

Figure 12

22

Figure 13

Figure 14

top of another. Orange might be produced by spreading transparent red over an opaque yellow. The resultant variety and brilliance was beyond anything that could be achieved by straight painting or by glazing in a single color over brown or gray underpainting. The uneven texture of piled-up light areas in the underpainting collects the fluid overpainting in its pits and shallows; a glaze may be applied over a large area and then rubbed off in spots. In scumbling, a technique in which a brush of thick, half-dry pigment is dragged over a dry, heavily textured area, the new color clings to the slightest roughness but allows the original color to show through in the shallows.

In the meantime the underpainting has a function beyond its first one of serving as a preliminary definition of form. If it is painted in golden browns it continues to affect the tonality of the completed picture in that direction; if it is done in black and white, the tonality is cooler, more silvery. In dark shadows the paint may be so thinly applied that we have hardly anything more than the original canvas dyed by the original underpainting; it is always in the lights that pigment is built up and heavily worked. In this technique shadows have a luminosity and vibrancy, no matter how dark they are, that cannot be achieved in earlier techniques.

This way of painting was adaptable to more restrained treatment also, as well as to exag-gerated treatments beyond Titian's. Caravaggio's *Musicians* (*Figure 12*; in color, Plate 70, Portfolio 6) is a meticulously executed painting that nevertheless owes its luminosity to underpainting and oil glazing. The texture, that is, the actual surface, of a painting is particularly difficult to reproduce accurately, but perhaps it is apparent in a full-size detail from *The Musicians* (Plate 105) that the red cloth here is first painted in the same way as the white cloth and then, in effect, "dyed" with a transparent crimson. It is probable that the shadows were touched with green along the edges to give a neutral tone, after glazing, between the red of the lights and the red-brown of the shadows.

Whereas Titian and Caravaggio capitalized on the sensuous and dramatically ornamental potentials of oil, Rembrandt found in it the means toward an opposite expression—mystery, melancholy, and philosophical brooding. His *Portrait of the Artist* (*Figure 13*) is typically Rembrandtian in the way forms emerge into brilliant light from the obscurity of warm shadow. A detail at full size (Plate 106) should show that Rembrandt's paint is progressively thicker and more opaque as the objects come into light. The areas of shadow are merely thin scrubs of paint; the lights are fat gobbets.

Modern Oil Techniques

The techniques of the old masters are not exactly lost, but after their abandonment it is not easy to pick them up again even from descriptions in records contemporary with the masters themselves. A variety of reasons account for their disappearance including so simple a thing as the appearance of oil paints ready-ground and emulsified with binder and purchaseable in tubes. At any rate the nineteenth century turned to "straight" painting. Paint was applied directly from the palette to the canvas without preliminaries of underpainting and without any systematic glazing. Since effects of great spontaneity and im-

Figure 15

mediacy are typical of "straight" painting at its best, it was adaptable to the nineteenth-century impressionist attitude of direct, unpretentious response to everyday subjects informally presented to the observer. For subject matter that was fragmentary in itself, a style of painting dependent on suggestion rather than on detailed statement was appropriate and in harmony with a very direct attack. Manet's *Boating* (*Figure 14*; in color, Plate 23, Portfolio 2) was discussed in this respect when we said that it offers us a kind of shorthand description of a woman's head, given here at full size (Plate 107). The entire passage was certainly painted all at once, with the "details," if we can call them that, brushed and spotted into freshly painted areas instead of being built up over preliminary foundations by glazes, scumbling, and the like.

If we compare this head with another, a half-size detail (Plate 108) from Picasso's *Woman in White* (*Figure 15*), we discover that, surprisingly, the modern archrevolutionist in painting draws more heavily from the past than Manet did. *Woman in White* is an arresting combination of paint textures involving building up in the lights of the face, glazing of a kind where the lower right section has been softened by a scrub of white, and a free, fluid calligraphic line indicating the fall of hair—all this

in connection with forms as highly simplified and as sharply defined as those in a tempera painting. In a picture like *Woman in White* we can find a little bit of nearly everything—a little bit of the classical past, a little bit of the Renaissance, a little bit of impressionism, even a suggestion of Chinese painting—in what we have called the calligraphic line of the hair, and, of course, a great deal of Picasso and our century.

But *Woman in White* is not a piece of craftsmanship in anything like the sense of the pictures we have been seeing in this portfolio. It is typical of the anarchic technique of contemporary painting, in which individual invention takes the place of systematic procedures. In discussing expressionism (Portfolio 3) we saw how Van Gogh used thick swirls of heavy paint as an essential expressive element in *The Starry Night* (Plate 25). His technique was altogether original, but "individual invention" may include as much reference to techniques of the past as the painter personally cares to make. Picasso frequently makes it in his own way, and among younger painters, at the moment, there are healthy indications of a return not exactly to painting methods of the old masters but to the idea that craftsmanship is a means toward expression rather than a brake upon it.

Notes on the Painters

Tommaso da Modena, 1325-1379, Italian

97. MADONNA AND CHILD (left panel of the MADONNA AND CHILD
    AND SAINT JEROME)

    *Tempera on wood. Height 11¾". The John G. Johnson Collection,
    Philadelphia*

Tommaso da Modena may or may not have painted the *Madonna and Child
and Saint Jerome* discussed in this portfolio. It is also attributed to an "unknown Sienese painter." One basis for the attribution to Tommaso da
Modena is the liveliness of the postures of the figures and the feeling for
vivacious narrative rather than formality. These qualities characterize his
most important work, a series of frescoes he painted in Treviso, Italy, in 1352.

Magdalen Master, XIII century, Italian

98. MADONNA ENTHRONED BETWEEN SAINTS PETER AND LEONARD,
    THIRD QUARTER XIII CENTURY

    *Tempera on canvas over wood. Height 42". Yale University Art
    Gallery, New Haven*

The painter of this impressive altarpiece is unknown; it would be a rare exception if its author could be identified. It is the work of one of the numerous
skilled painter-craftsmen who are distinguishable from one another only by
very fine points of style, since they worked in a time when our concept of a
painter as a strong individualist was unknown. There were certain standards
of sound craftsmanship that a painter had to meet, just as there were standards of sound craftsmanship that a carpenter or a stonemason or a jeweler had
to meet. The painter met them, and the satisfaction he found in his work had
nothing much to do with the idea of personal expression; that was to develop
later.

Domenico Ghirlandaio, 1449-1494, Italian

99. Head of Teodoro from FRANCESCO SASSETTI AND HIS SON TEODORO, 1472

Tempera on wood. Height of detail 10½". The Metropolitan Museum of Art, Jules S. Bache Collection, 1949

Ghirlandaio was one of the busiest of the painters who appeared in such unprecedented numbers in Florence in the fifteenth century. Several of his colleagues have figured in preceding portfolios of this series. Lacking the grandeur of Masaccio, the subtlety of Botticelli, and certainly the genius of Leonardo, Ghirlandaio occupies a firm position in that second rank of extremely skillful painters who supplied a dependable product meant to satisfy the insatiable appetite of wealthy Florentine families for portraits and mural decorations. He is the pure and perfect example of the renaissance artist-craftsman, the product of a system of training in which a painter learned his craft according to an accumulated tradition of fine workmanship, and then, since this was the Renaissance and an age of invention and individuality, added to it whatever he had to offer in the way of individual expression. But Ghirlandaio did not have a great deal to offer—he lacked imagination. Still, it is refreshing that he never strove to go beyond himself; his very pedestrianism makes for a kind of honesty and directness that can be a virtue in itself.

He was the most objective of realists, seldom venturing a comment on the subjects he painted. The suggestion of sentiment in our charming study of the old man and the little boy is more inherent in the subjects themselves than contributed interpretatively by the artist. This is a typical Ghirlandaio portrait, with its clear, crisp definition of the sitters' features and a nice attention to details of costume, especially when they are adaptable to decorative treatment.

Ghirlandaio was a phenomenally productive muralist. As such he was first of all a decorator of walls, not an interpreter of a story nor an observer of man and man's fate. His best-known murals ornament the choir of Santa Maria Novella in Florence. Nominally, their subject matter is religious; actually, they show us fashionable Florentine interiors peopled by Ghirlandaio's patrons and their friends, most of them identifiable, going through their paces as the characters in a religious narrative, or simply standing around to look on.

Andrea Mantegna, 1431-1506, Italian

100. Joseph from THE ADORATION OF THE SHEPHERDS, ABOUT 1460

Tempera transferred from wood to canvas. Height of detail 10½". The Metropolitan Museum of Art, anonymous gift, 1932

In the art of Mantegna, who has already been discussed in the Notes on the Painters in Portfolio 7, there is an element of fantasy, of the supernatural, that gives his work much of its curious intensity. It is found in the curiously shaped rock formations of many colors, in his blighted and split trees sprouting sudden luxuriant growths of new foliage, and in the magically detailed clarity of his distances, where the tiniest object is revealed as if the eye were a powerful telescope. He is most at home with subjects of violence or cruelty; Christian subjects give full play to this aspect of his art in scenes of the martyrdoms of saints. But as *The Adoration of the Shepherds* shows, he can also adapt his style to gentler subjects. The atmosphere of quiet that fills this picture is not the usual one of half-sad serenity most artists liked to give to The Adoration, but rather one of enchanted stillness where every object and every detail of every object, each fold of cloth, each pebble, each leaf, seems transfixed within crystal.

Carlo Crivelli, active by 1457—died after 1495, Italian

101. Angel from PIETÀ, 1473-74

Tempera on wood. Height of detail 9¾". The John G. Johnson Collection, Philadelphia

Crivelli, a contemporary of Mantegna, achieved what would seem to be the impossible: he exaggerated the crisp, hard modeling of the Paduan school, which would seem incapable of further exaggeration. The edges of Crivelli's forms are like the edges of razors. Expressively, he goes beyond intensity to something close to hysteria. In the end, however, this exaggeration becomes a formula, and like all formulas it frequently rings hollow. Crivelli's manner is repetitious and sometimes seems an affectation, yet he remains a fascinating painter. Like many other painters who have adopted an extreme manner, he depends a great deal upon pure decorative attraction. His pictures are full of ornamental swags of fruit and vegetables, strongly patterned fabrics, and architectural curiosities. Frequently he amazes us by introducing actual textures along with his simulated ones. In the *Pietà* in this portfolio his exaggeration is quite obvious in the fantastic grimaces of the mourning angels, the sinuous patterning of locks of hair, and the morbid emphasis on the wounds in Christ's hands and side.

Giovanni Bellini, about 1430-1516, Italian

102. PORTRAIT OF A YOUNG MAN

Tempera and oil on wood. Height 10½". The Metropolitan Museum of Art, Jules S. Bache Collection, 1949

Giovanni Bellini, his brother Gentile (1429-1507), and his father Jacopo (1400-1470) were Venetian painters whose work covers the development of that school from its primitive style to the verge of its climax in Titian. This development is even evident within the work of Giovanni alone. His earliest paintings are precise, crisp, and realistic; a strong resemblance to those of his contemporary and brother-in-law Mantegna is apparent during one period, but Bellini always modifies a little the extraordinary hardness of the Paduan master. During an extraordinarily long life he painted a prodigious number of pictures and was never content to settle into a manner. His development is consistently in the direction of greater gentleness and grace, expressed through his study of the nature of light as a unifying factor in painting. In his final work he touches the spirit of the High Renaissance in Venice with its poetic fullness, its opulence, its glowing lights and rich shadows. Giorgione and Titian were his pupils. No other painter can match him in span, and it would be hard to find another whose level of achievement was consistently higher.

Simon Marmion, 1425-1489, French

103. Soldiers from THE CRUCIFIXION, 1470

Oil and tempera on wood. Height of detail 25". The John G. Johnson Collection, Philadelphia

The most important work of Marmion, a painter who apparently exerted a strong influence during his lifetime, has been lost and very little is known about him. The works known to be his or attributable to him with some certainty show, like *The Crucifixion*, a great delicacy and at the same time great certainty of execution, a lively invention of ornamental forms (of architecture or costume), and a kind of gentle elegance of spirit.

Titian (Tiziano Vecelli), 1477-1576, Italian

104. Detail from VENUS AND ADONIS

Oil on canvas. Height of detail 18". The Metropolitan Museum of Art, Jules S. Bache Collection, 1949

In Titian the Venetian school reaches its climax. A pupil of Bellini, he lived, like his master, to a very great age and painted constantly throughout his adult life. Bellini brought Venetian painting from its primitive realism to the poetic, idyllic, sensuous mood thought of as its most characteristic expression. With his friend Giorgione, Titian as a young painter reflects this mood. After Giorgione's early death Titian's art continued to ripen, becoming more sensuous and more worldly. He developed the technique of oil painting to its maximum potential in richness of texture and opulence of color. In his old age broad, full forms already apparent in *Venus and Adonis* are painted even more freely. The old man's failing eyesight and the waning precision of his hand could not obliterate his lifelong experience with form and color. Although outlines soften and details vanish into the crumbling brilliance of light or rich, mysterious shadows, the power of the forms and the structure of their compositional relationships is not weakened. In these very late paintings Titian anticipated some of the effects of nineteenth-century impressionism.

Titian led a princely life. The friend of the great men of his time, he was revered as the greatest painter of his day.

Michelangelo Merisi da Caravaggio, 1573-1610, Italian

105. Hand of the lute player from THE MUSICIANS, 1594-95

Oil on canvas. Height of detail 10½". The Metropolitan Museum of Art, Rogers Fund, 1952

Caravaggio was a revolutionary painter in his use of exaggerated chiaroscuro and extreme realism. *The Musicians*, however, is typical of his earlier, more poetic spirit, not only more gentle in mood but less highly dramatized than his later work. For further notes on Caravaggio, see Portfolio 6.

Rembrandt Harmensz. van Ryn, 1606-1669, Dutch

106. Detail from PORTRAIT OF THE ARTIST, 1660

Oil on canvas. Height of detail 10½". The Metropolitan Museum of Art, bequest of Benjamin Altman, 1913

Rembrandt, like Caravaggio, forced chiaroscuro to its limits for dramatic emphasis, and, like Titian, he made the surface texture of his painting a part of the creation of light's vibrancy. But unlike either of these Italians he put these techniques into the service of the melancholy of the North, into an introspective, even tragic, statement of man's mind and soul. This, at any rate, is true of his later work. For further notes on Rembrandt, see Portfolio 7.

Edouard Manet, 1832-1883, French

107. Head of the woman from BOATING

Oil on canvas. Height of detail 11⅝". The Metropolitan Museum of Art, H. O. Havemeyer Collection, 1929

Manet was the first martyr of "modern art." His painting, which today is so immediately attractive and could not possibly seem shocking, was howled down during his lifetime by critics and a public who demanded the rather stuffy, sentimentalized realism to which they were accustomed in the painting of official hacks. Paintings like *Boating*, with its brilliant economy, were considered crude, incompetent, and even insulting to a public for whom any departure from the most conventional way of painting was incomprehensible. For further notes on Manet, see Portfolio 2.

Pablo Picasso, born 1881, Spanish

108. Head from WOMAN IN WHITE, 1923

Oil on canvas. Height of detail 20". The Metropolitan Museum of Art, Rogers Fund, 1951

Picasso is certainly the best-known living painter and is probably more celebrated in his own day than any other painter who has ever lived. His fantastic career covers so many different styles that it would take columns to list them with only brief descriptions. Though most people think first of Picasso as a painter of the wildest abstractions, he has from time to time worked in more conventional ways. One of his most surprising shifts of manner is represented in *The Woman in White*. After the extreme distortions of cubism he reverted briefly to the monumentality of classicism, making of course his own highly personal adaptation of it. For further notes on Picasso, see Portfolio 4.